My Name is Resilience

T. Michelle

ISBN: 979-8-9864516-5-7

DEDICATION

To the people who were cannonballed into my life when I needed you the most, thank you. Words can never express how grateful I am to have you in my tribe.

What a Beautiful Baby

The softness of her skin
The love in her eyes
The sweetness of her look
What a beautiful baby
So soundly she sleeps
So contently she plays
What a beautiful baby
So lucky am I to have her
So blessed am I to keep her
So willingly to love her
Oh what a beautiful baby
Gave birth to her so quickly
She'll grow up so fast
Someday she'll leave home
As a beautiful young lady
-Mom

Youth

The Rainbow of a Rose

The rainbow of a rose
The beauty of the earth
The smell of the rain
The dirt on my shirt

Taken for granted
These beautiful things
Without even thinking
This powerful lesson leaves

The influence of a friend
The hug from a mother
The nod of understanding
The singing song of another

Meditation taken for granted
Like happiness thrown out to sea
No wonder all the serious faces
And boring lives have we

Peace

Peace
Quiet, relaxing
Hush, listen, and sleep
Serenity, grace, dance, dusk
Peace

Small Town

Life slows down, time to breathe
Windows open, in comes the breeze
The only sound, crickets speak
A cloudless sky, endless stars peek

Leaves rustle in the trees
No cars speeding by
Only peace felt as the street sleeps
The quiet silence echoes outside

Living in a small town
Often has its perks
Fields stretch all around
It's rare that chaos be found

Asking for sugar
Unlocked doors
The community there
Always yours

Where friends become family
Extending beyond the shores
Pick each other up
Open the doors

My Prayer

Thank you father
For another day to live
Thank you father
For the immense love I have to give

Thank you father
For the people who walked into my life
To teach me, to guide me
To give me safety so I can thrive

Thank you father
For the strength I have been given
Thank you father
For the comfort, come from heaven

Thank you father
For the sings that you are real
For strengthening my faith
To be as strong as the toughest steel

I know there have been times
Where I haven't quite listened
I apologize for the moments
My choices weren't what you envisioned

I pray that I may follow
The path that leads back to thee
To be the very best person
That I could ever be

I pray I may follow your example
And treat others just the same
To love and support and forever cherish
As others have done to me

Dear Father as I end
This prayer I give to thee
That others will feel the very same love
That I, everyday, continue to see

My Name is Resilience

My name is Resilience
I was born to shine
To survive the hottest fire
And somehow remain kind

I've been beaten down and broken
I've climbed from the abyss
I've climbed that very mountain cliff
To be able to see a view like this

I've found a way to thrive
When the wind slashes my face
I've cut my way through the jungle
And learned to show myself grace

I am simply human
I will continue to grow
Through life I remain resilient
Even if the future is unknown

Little Girl

The girl with the big, blue eyes
The brunette locks and curls
The one that grew up too fast
In an ever-racing world

She'll live her life in fear
She will feel forever small
She protects herself from fate
And pins herself against the wall

The ringing in her ears
The inability to breathe
The world is no longer safe
Craving peace feels like greed

She'll skip through the fields
Wander through the trees
Splash through any pond
And enjoy the calming breeze

The world slows, the catches her breath
She finds the fork in her road
And leans in to smell the flowers
While she climbs the rocky slopes

As a Child

As a child we are born
Into a world so unknown
Forgetting everything that happened before
So clouded, so alone

As a child we grow and learn
Everything we know and see
From the food our mother cooks
To the flowers and the trees

As a child we learn to become
The person we will eventually be
Sometimes we take the spirit of our elders
Sometimes we simply need to break free

As a child we are molded
By family, teachers, and friends so dear
Words and comfort and wisdom found
Everything we have needed to hear

As a child we always wish to be grown
To see the world through different eyes
Until we find that our best memories
Are imagining shapes of the clouds in the sky

As a human when we grow
We forget that feeling of being carefree
What it means to be a child
While, imaginative, and free

Worry

Little girl
Eyes red with tears
Awake, late at night
Being bombarded with all her fears

Sitting in her little princess bed
No one knows the tears she will cry
Worry that's building walls around her heart
Or the endless moments she's asking why

A stalwart face, this little girl wears
To not draw to herself any attention
Stay strong, don't be weak
That pain you have, don't ever mention

Silence

Silence is golden, everybody says
But sometimes it is not
That darkness creeps inside
Even though it's peace that we sought

Every once in a while, it's beautiful
That quiet, soulful place
If it's done right, we may find ourselves
And all the internal struggle may cease

But we must be careful, you see
For if we are not, we can then be trapped
Set in our ways, set in our mind
And all that silence builds
Until we can no longer adapt

Silence can sometimes be
More isolated than you think
How are we supposed to connect
And make sure we don't sink

Darkness

Feeling So Much

Life can be excruciatingly hard
When you don't know what to do
Just moving forward is as hard as a rock
But slowly I am moving through

Optimism and peace I have always felt
Right now those feelings are askew
I've found a way to learn to cope
When the tornadoes come through

Who knew all these emotions
Could plunge one into the depths of the sea
I'm trying to keep my head above water
But some days all I can do is scream

I Need Help, I Don't Know What to Do

This is getting so tiring
I don't want to do this anymore
The pain and suffering, I know it's all for good
But I've been at this for far too long

I don't know what to do
I really do need help
My mind keeps telling me no
I don't know what to do

I can't go on if I have to live this way
I really do need help
I'm sick of struggling through the rough days
The lingering panic makes me throw up

I very much want to live
But I can't do this myself
I hate living like this
I really do need help

I know we have to struggle
I know life can't be easy
But some days I can't get out of bed
I just hurt, so badly

I don't know what to do
When life falls apart, I hurt, I panic
By body seizes up, I panic more
I can't think, I can't talk

No one knows what's going on
Everything crumples to the ground
Nauseousness overwhelms me
Terror fills my eyes when I shake so hard

I get so afraid it will kill me
Before I have a chance to fight back
I need help, so badly
But I don't know how to ask

Never Stop Fighting

Never stop fighting
Never lose hope
Don't think about giving up
Keep walking down that road

It's going to be hard
disappointing at times
But need to know
That you are worth it

You fight that fight
You learn to hit back
Whatever struggle you face
You can rise above

Never stop breathing, never give up
Your worth is more than you could dream
Don't let your brain fool you into losing
Don't dare walk out of that ring

No matter how dark it becomes
Or how suffocating it gets
You can crawl out of this
You won't drown anymore
Or take anymore hits

Sometimes I Feel

Sometimes I truly feel
Like I've lost all control
All I can do is sit back
And let life tear apart my soul

That awful mindset I'm in
I feel like I'm so alone
I can't help but shut down
To become a robot, become unknown

The panic, the fear, the anger
Becomes so overwhelming
Constantly knocking me to my knees
Draining everything

If I Die Young

I have often thought
About my impending doom
What my life would be
If I wasn't in the room

I have watched stories
People who never gave up hope
Who kept their loved ones here on Earth
Because they didn't know how to cope

If my brain has already gone
Give me a hug and say goodbye
My soul has left, my body needs rest
I will be watching from the sky

Take my words, read them often
Remember who I was, who I wanted to be
Take my possessions, give them away
Feel the emotions, take my reach

Keep my memories simple
Leave the fancy things at home
Simply lay me in the ground
Cover up my tomb

No One Feels What I Feel

No one feels the guilt that I feel
When I do something wrong
That nagging, that aching
I'm not that strong

I look all around me
I'm the only one not the same
If they knew the feelings I feel
A monster who should be shamed

I sometimes feel solace
With those whom I've shared my story
Nuggets of peace and hope
Faith and glory

No one feels what I feel
A toxic thought that plagued me
So long that I eventually believed
There was nothing good to see

I wasn't strong, I wasn't me
Was I just wasting breath?
I don't often talk of that dark, dark place
It often included that of my own death

No one feels what I feel
But I am not alone
Eventually my mind will conquer that fight
The power of that statement overthrown

Hidden From the Outside

It never seems that girl has anything wrong
She must be so blessed
Never does anyone expect the heartache
Settling inside her chest

It never seems real, the pain she endures
The life she lives is hidden from the world
She keeps herself safe from the outsiders' gaze
And the horrible threats they may hurt

Only those she grew to trust
Will ever know and understand her mind
You'll never see the walls she built
The ones that keep everyone blind

Broken

I woke up this morning
Feeling completely broken
I felt like my heart had been washed away
Sucked into a black hole of sin

I haven't felt like this for a while
I have done everything I can
I prayed to God it would leave
It's tearing me apart again

For some reason, in a split second, it's gone
The emptiness is filled with ecstasy
Although not for very long
It seems being broken is my destiny

My life is spent almost living in fear
In fear of waking up in darkness
A darkness that never dawns
And I wither away, no longer to exist

Reality Hits

Everything is becoming so real
It's hard to take it all in
What I have gone through, everything I've done
What will it all amount to?

I will very soon be grown
And my life will drastically change
I only hope those feelings won't come back
I'll do anything in exchange

I don't know what I will do, what I will face
I think I'm prepared for it all
No, I don't know what is going to happen
If I ever fall

I know that I am so much stronger now
But there's always that risk of me falling again
I worry about so many things
How did I handle things then?

The future, no one knows what it'll have in store
And we can't dwell in the past
The only thing we can do is live in the present
Life passes by so fast

Promise

Endless promises are made
In this life we all share
Some broken and shattered
By those who don't care

Some promises however, protected and pure
Supported by hope and light
By those angels who swoop into our lives
When we want to give up that fight

I promise you it gets better
This life is not done
It's never too late
To pick up the pace and run

I promise you it's worth it
Every bump, every bruise
I know that dreaded, dark misery you feel
But I promise you, it's not a ruse

Never Wanna Leave

We haven't spoken for a while now
Just glances, waves, and off we go
Every once in a while we have a few words
Only enough to show we've grown

When we were together, I always felt calm
A place where I felt safe
I wanted to stay because I know
There would be brightness not far away

I had someone that I knew would listen
And hugged me when I was down
You helped me through all my trials
You made my life seem sound

I know someday I need to grow
Take my own steps, and stretch my own wings
But I know whenever I need that calm
I have a place I never wanna leave

Hope

To You

To the one who changed my life
And the one to whom my life was saved
To the times I wanted to give up
And the fights I came out unscathed

To the ones to brought me true peace
To the one who gave me grace
To the times I broke into a million shattered bits
And the moments I set the world ablaze

To the people that rescued my heart
May you feel the gratitude I share
And the moments upon which I am made
With humility to you may I swear

To the times I had fallen to the dark
May I shake your hand and bid thee farewell
To the light that has filled my soul
May I humbly bow to your presence
And no longer be unwell

There are no words to express my thanks
No actions to pay you back
But may I walk forward, and for others fight
And strength and resilience, no longer lack

I Wish

There are some things in my life
That I wish I could change
Something I would do differently
To protect myself from the mange

At points, willpower and self-control
Disappeared at the sound of a snap
Keeping me inside this darkness
In a way sitting on the devil's lap

I wish my life were different sometimes, but
I am grateful for the life I have
Because I am stronger than I have ever been
And there's never too much time to laugh

I wish, I wish, upon a shooting star
Wherever I may be
To be able to know who I am
And who I want to be

To be able to let others see who I really am
No matter which side of me they need
To be strong, to be my own soul
And lead the life I truly want to lead

You Were Never There

You never cared about my feelings
You pushed me way too hard
You took everything I cared about most
You were never there for me

You took my strength to speak
You isolated my mind
You were always filled with hate
You were never there for me

So I'm not who you want me to be
But stop treating me like you are
You will never have the power you crave
You're not there for me

You made me feel like running away
You made me want to take my own life
You made me terrified of my own self
You're not there for me

You don't listen, you don't care
You ruined my self esteem
As I pick up the pieces, I realize what you did
You will never be there for me

Conflict

Crazy people do crazy things
To stand for what they believe
But for me, every time I try
Nothing will let me achieve

I try to act
I try to speak
But it feels no one
No one is listening to me

I'm all alone in this big bad world
Something I feel so alone
I just want to cry
Some days, bad habits are so hard to forgo

Sometimes I feel like giving up
Temptation gets the best of me
But I'll try and try again
Until I finally succeed

Confusion and sadness
Is interfering with the happiness I once had
The roller coaster is starting again
How to I remember emotions past

The world spins around and around
Not bothering to stop for me or you
But just hanging on to life
Is not an easy chore to do

Why is life so hard
Why am I too weak to hold on
Why does everything keep crashing down
When I'm just starting to move on

Times have passed by oh so fast
Yet I remember every mistake
I wish I could forget all of that
So some sort of peace of mind I can take

There's so much conflict
Passing through my mind
How do I continue to move forward
And breathe through the endless grind

Pain

The pain was unbearable
I pray it is worth it
The circles, the panic, the screams in my head
I don't have enough grit

I try to rise up each day
But I always end up on my knees
I hear the screams inside my head
Scared and unable to breathe

Some days, it's hard to move
I feel completely paralyzed
I want to give up, but I can't
There's gotta be something more, right?

Plead for Help

Please help me to not be scared
Please help me through this
Please help me hang on
I want to go, I'm not going to be missed

Everything is spinning faster
The whole world is crashing down
How do I cope? What do I do?
Let me lay under the dirt, under this mound

I don't want to do this anymore
I can't breathe
There's a light somewhere, I know it
But it doesn't feel like that light is for me

No More Superman

At times, the clock seems to stand still
Yet there is no time to dream
When I finally have a moment to breathe
Pushed underwater, forced to drown it seems

No matter how well I balance things out
I'm gifted with more to do
Once I find time to take care of myself
I'm taking care of everyone else too

I can no more be Superman
I need my own time now
I wonder if I'm the one who's not ready to leave
Or if others can't let me go

To Think

To think I let myself fall
So far into those depths
So far I couldn't see
There was somewhere to go next

To thin I let myself stay
In a place that burned my soul
Enough for there to be a wall
That kept me from every feasible goal

I was comfortable, I was safe
My mind would always stay
Yet it was the fear of falling
That kept me stuck, holding that weight

I never looked at the big picture
The full scene
That staying for what I loved
Meant giving up my peace

To think that at one time I told myself
I wasn't allowed to grow
Because I needed to stay where it was safe
To do all I can to lay low

To think that I held myself back
Because my brain was so sick
But no longer will I hide
This newfound power is going to stick

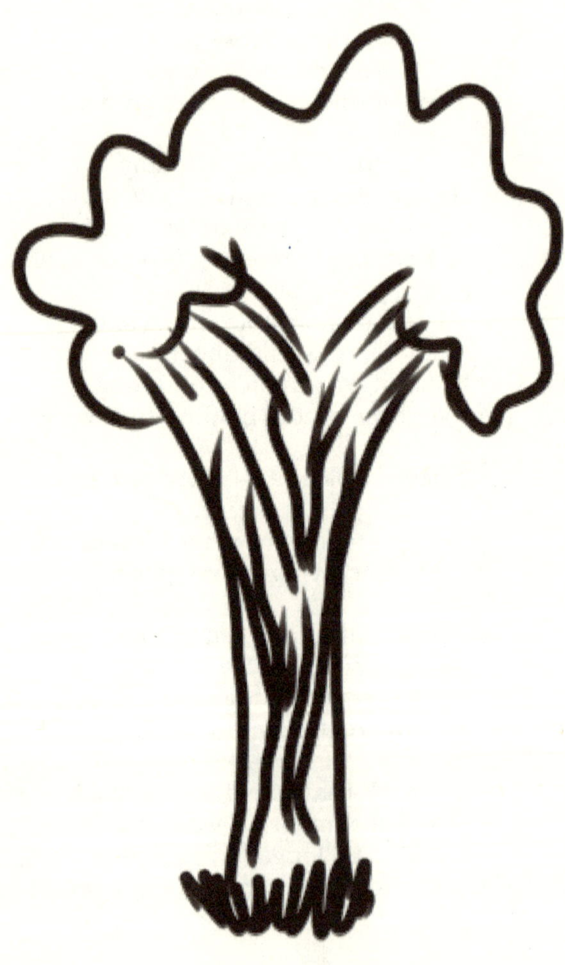

Superhero

I wanna take their pain away
Rescue them from their hurt
To be a crutch when they cannot stand
To pick them up from the dirt

I will gladly give myself
To grab my cape and fly
I won't even wait for their signal
And I'll stay until they can get by

I once believed I had superpowers
I never once thought to pull back
The power to protect the mind
To fix a world that was sad

I stand on the sidelines
And watch the fires burn
Knowing how I cant save
The ashes from the urn

I have to be my own superhero
At least for some time
To find my true identity
Before I think to save mankind

Find Your Voice and Speak

When you feel there is nowhere to go
When you feel powerless
Reach deep down inside your heart
Take a step back and give yourself space

Find that voice you've kept inside
Locked away in a box
Speak aloud what's in your heart, on your mind
Stop carrying those heavy rocks

Don't be afraid of the words you will say
Of course, it's easier said than done
What worries you, what scares you
Those thoughts you can't outrun

Find that beautiful voice and speak
Loud, brave, and proud
Free yourself from the power of the dark
And untie that suffocating shroud

Magic Miracles

I open my eyes each morning
Grateful to have another day
I've seen more than I ever dreamed
I don't know what else to say

These miracles are like magic
In every sense of the word
How did the magician find the right card
It has to be a trick for sure

But it's not a trick
It's very very real
I see these miracles every single day
Being alive is a miracle to me

Gentle Touch

The warmth of a tender hug
When my world is falling apart
The safety of that embrace
Melting together the wounds of my injured heart

Holding me tight when I am shaking
Making the world seem not so big
Assuring me you heard my silent screams
Unconditionally loving me and removing my wig

The wig I wear, to make myself look strong
The one people see
But you know that wig hides the truth
That I simply just want to be free

He's There

When life is crashing down, beating you up
The first step is to pray
When you can't get up, can't breathe
He's there every step of the way

I've often felt completely alone
When my racing thoughts take flight
Little did I know
I'm never out of his sight

I know now that I am unstoppable
Knowing who's behind me
A power that's beyond this world
Countless tender mercies I see

Forward

Because of Faith

I have come so, so far
Farther than I ever thought
So much I've learned and done
Everything is falling into place

I'm finally gaining back
All that I've lost
My mindset is changing again for the better
Even if it seems such a high cost

It's sure amazing how far I've come
Every blessing I've been given
My life being the most precious
My eyes will always glisten

Broken Walls

You sat and listened to me ramble on
And were willing to hear my story
You asked relentless questions
And planted the seeds I needed to sow

You made me speak
And think of what I was going to say
You've told me countless times
That I would indeed be okay

Thank you for being there for me
For making me smile, for making me laugh
For the hugs and the comfort
For the love I needed to have

You broke down so many walls
You always knew what to say
You helped me discover me
In a time where everything felt grey

You saw inside of me
So much that I couldn't see
You pushed me to be better
And taught me that I wasn't weak

I Can't Wait

I will be so happy
I will feel so free
A burden lifted off my shoulders
A burden I no longer have to see

I'll walk into that office
Just as nervous as ever
But I know when I ask that question
My life will be changed forever

I've never asked for this much help before
In a sense I'm nervous and scared
I just don't want to get hurt
Part of me still felt nobody cared

This time is different
There's no reason to be afraid
This is something I have to do
Because for a long time I've strayed

I can't wait until everything falls into place
I can't wait until I can finally stretch
I can't wat until I can reach for the sky
Without the risk of falling off the edge

I can't wait to be able to tell my story
To grow stronger than I thought I could be
One with an amazing happy ever after
One that right now, I cannot see

The Next Step

The next step on the journey I'm taking
Is asking for the help I need now
I've wanted it for a while
But asking for it, I really didn't know how

The power I feel now, those walls torn down
The ones I've had up for far too long
It feels so amazing but I'll admit
Af first it felt so wrong

I felt so vulnerable, I felt so weak
Those walls disguised themselves as strengths
Then the feelings passed, I realized that power
Hidden from me since I was young

New discoveries I found about myself
New discoveries about the world around me
Only made me so much stronger, happier
A new light I can now see

What Do You See?

Look over at the mucky lake
Filthy water, sharp rocks all around
Maybe a wildlife refuge
So animals may be safe and sound

There's the child sitting alone
Who seems to have no friends
Maybe a future president
Or a wonderful hand he can lend

The positive in the painful gravel
We sometimes don't see in the strife
We forget to take a moment, stand still
Ask "What do you see?" in this busy life

Panic Attack

I can't breathe, I can't think
I don't know what to do
The anger, the panic
Makes my head explode

Uncontrollable shaking, the blackouts
Dizzy beyond belief
My brain gets so screwed up
My function turns to grief

There's no hiding when it comes
It gets worse each and every time
I can't speak, can't ask for help
I go thru hell thinking I'm fine

The pain I endure, the worry on my face
I never know how much I can take
I see the fire, I drown the sea
In a split second, I break

I Can't Concentrate

So many things have happened,
Some things I felt I couldn't pull through
Events I've had to watch
Times where I didn't know what to do

Watching people fall apart
Make me do the same
People like us who didn't want to live any longer
And the people we chose to blame

I hate being like this
And enduring life at the same time
Why do I have to feel this way
Feeling like I've committed a crime

If you are hearing this now
I need help, please pray
Because I am doing the same
Just trying to get through the day

Emotion Coaster

So many things to do
So little time
Theres a roller coaster spinning around
And I can't see the line

I am worrying about so many things
Things that before have never crossed my mind
Reality will soon hit me hard
Peace and comfort I am desperate to find

I am so scared and tired
Feeling discouraged too
I can't feel the darkness from long ago
I feel like it'll be here soon

I'm trying to empower myself
To keep myself from going back
But it is so hard to feel pleased
With something I'm afraid to look at

I sometimes wish my life wasn't like this
Why do I feel this way
When it doesn't work, it won't let me in
This can't be my fate

Turmoil

I don't know what goes through my head
I feel like I'm spinning in circles
Up and down, near and far
The nonstop coaster makes me want to hurl

I've always hidden my turmoil from others
I'm worried they would think I'm weak
I have changed so much since I started here
People know now, those secrets have leaked

I always sell myself short
I forget how strong I can be
Even when I've shown how much I've grown
I cower away from the darkness that be

The constant turmoil in my mind
Thousands of thoughts and screams
I'm drowning in a pool of all the voices
My reality bursting at the seams

Please just give me a moment to breathe
A chance to stand on my feet
I'm afraid that again I will fall
Face first on the cold, hard concrete

I am Tired

I am so tired
So very very tired
Why do I have to do this again
My soul you have already acquired

I don't want to do this anymore
I just want this to be over
I feel so very sick
I can't possibly fall any lower

Why do I have to keep doing this
How long do I have to keep going
I'm getting near to my edge
That white towel I am thinking of throwing

I'm trying my best to endure to the end
But I don't know how much more I can take
Please, I need help
The stress keeps making me shake

Existence

This existence is so agonizing
Because I have to deal with this pain
Sometimes I've felt like running away
But any attempt to escape would be in vain

Because if I run, I have to hide
And eventually, the will find me
The pain, the screams, get louder and louder
What does it feel like to be free?

When they do, they will yell and scream
I do not have the courage to run away
I feel stuck, pinned down, suffocating
I feel so, so weak

Inner Demons

It's been hard to conquer the inner demons
The ones that try to take over
The ones that try to destroy
I can't feel any lower

Some days, I can't get out of bed
Crawled up into a ball
I'm not myself
I don't know who I've become at all

Everything seizes up
I can't move
I can't function with this pain
What am I supposed to do

Sometimes I wish I could just start shaking
And not stop until the pain went away
It's been hard fighting these feelings
It's a feeling I can't quite explain

These inner demons come and go as they please
Sometimes they try to destroy me
I wish I could just disappear
But then those demons... disappear

Then everything changes
The sun shines again
The brightness and joy are only
temporary
Until those demons attack, amen

Pause

Why does life keep falling apart
When I think I'm on the right track
It keeps breaking into pieces
As soon as I've filled in the cracks

I've just gotten my strength enough to stand
That tunnel keeps looking so bleak
How can I continue to be strong
When I'm being kicked where I'm weak?

Easily I've gotten so sick
When I've only started to heal
One step forward, two steps back
I don't know anymore what to feel

I just need to breathe
To pause for just a second
What am I supposed to learn
When my weaknesses become a weapon

I Understand Now

I understand now why we are different
Why someone lives this way or that
No one has the same mind
We all have a different world on our back

the reason why we are this way
is so we can learn from each other
i understand how a voice can change lives
i understand we are all each other's brother

I understand now why I am here today
I understand what all I can do
I understand now why I am the way I am
Because of all I've been through

Gratitude

Lesson

One of the greatest lessons in life
You can't go at it alone
No matter how hard you try
You never find the perfect tone

If I asked for help, I was weak
It's what I always thought
Once I gave up that nonexistent control
I realized the door was never shut

I found my power
I finally found peace
I learned what safety really was
At last I felt seen

There's something missing from this world
Community and compassion gone
We're supposed to care for each other
Enough of "my side won"

We've lost sight of our fellow man
It seems we can't find our way back
But we can't walk alone
How do we get back on track?

Never Settle

Never settle for anything less
Than the best you could ever be
Never let a hill get in the way
Of the million dollar view you wish to see

There is a mountain in the way
An entire world on the other side
We train our entire lives for that climb
We just need to find the best guide

Never settle for a complacent seat
When you could fly the plane
Grow into your power, deep inside
You were born to travel against the grain

Wouldn't Change My Life

There is absolutely nothing about my life
That I would ever want to change
Although I wish things were different sometimes
I wouldn't have it any other way

Without everything happening how it has
I wouldn't be where I am now
I know most days won't be my best
Each day I breathe, I try to grow

I'm so grateful for every day I live
Each day I can take a breath
Each day becomes a week, each week a month
Months becomes years, I finally embrace death

My life has been rocky
And at times very dark
There's nothing that would make me change
It's gotten me where I am

Never More Than Now

It's been so long since I've heard your voice
Since I've seen your crooked smile
I cherish the memories when I was young
It's hard to imagine
You've been gone a while

A huge part of me is now missing
It's been hard to walk on my own
All I want to do is speak to you
To tell you how much I've grown

I hope you are proud of me
For doing the best I can
To carry on your beautiful legacy
And all the miles I have ran

Nevermore than now have I wanted
To feel your loving embrace
You were taken from us far too soon
And with a great amount of haste

I watched as your soul left
And your body gave in
The world was turned to a shade of grey
That light in me for a while, dimmed

Nevermore than now have I needed your help
Your wisdom to get through this life
But whenever I dig into the memories
The pain still stabs like a knife

I often feel you with me
I've seen you in my dreams
I can only hope I'll see you again
Any day, by any means

Advice, My Daughter

Walk in the grass
Bask in the sun
Make the biggest cannonballs
Grab the ice cream when you're done

Pave your own path
Make your own way
If others choose to follow
Invite them to play

Listen to others
Understand their mind
Connect the dots
Wisdom you will find

Splash in that puddle
Learn something new
Go explore the world
Watch the flowers bloom

Fight for your life
Protect your peace
Don't be afraid to speak
But for yourself have grace

You're stronger than you know
Your ancestors cheering you on
Find your hidden power
Sing your powerful song

Create your own magic
Share it with the world
Show nothing but kindness
Softly carry your beautiful pearls

There may be one you come across
Who cannot speak
Please fight for others
In those times, don't be weak

Look back on your life
See where you've come
Be proud of who you are
And loudly pound your drum

Soften those beautiful eyes
Stand tall, shoulders back
Never be anything but genuine
And know that strength you can never lack

Thanks Dear Friend

Thank you dear friend
Or listening so well
Thank you dear friend
For helping me pull through

You've made such an impact
On this life
No matter where you go
You'll always be a hero of mine

Thank you dear friend
For simply being you
Thank you dear friend
For letting me be me

Thank you dear friend
For the notes you wrote
Thank you dear friend
For the calls you made

Thank you dear friend for listening
When I needed you the most
When I needed you to stand me on my feet
Thank you dear friend for everything

Strength

When one holds thine head up high
In the midst of the battle winds
When battered and bruised with nowhere to go
When evil overthrows and faith thins

Clenching your fists, letting out a mighty roar
Pushing back the burning walls
You will conquer your struggle
You'll win your fight, and evil will fall

Just as one with cancer goes into remission
Or one once bullied gains the most success
One who speaks when no one will
Or lend a hand after a broken heart
Making it hurt less

Strength is a brave face in the brunt of adversity
Strength is the ability to let go and cry
Strength is getting back up after a mighty blow
Strength is the capability to simply let go

I watch the toll this all takes
By the exhaustion on your face
But one thing I see is the light of our heart
Filled with strength and grace

Branching Out

The roots of a tree grow deep and strong
Nothing can blow it away
Storms can brew, winds may rage
The tree stays in its place

Branches grow, flowers bloom
Waving at the sun in the sky
Then hide away and shiver
When they see the lightning strikes

The rings expand, the roots thicken
The green leaves breathing away
Growing stronger forever and ever
With each passing wave

Branches break sometimes
Once in a while giving in
The bark crackles, hear a snap
When the storm seems grim

Roots continue to spread
The trunk bracing for impact
Then the clouds part, the sun rise
The tree continues to stand tall

I Will Win

I remember you like it was yesterday
The day you broke me apart
Ripped my soul into a thousand pieces
The day you ripped out my heart

I was overwhelmed, scared
The world starting to spin
The only things I heard were a thousand
screams
I was spread so thin

I can't do this, I can't win
There's no way I'm strong enough
These words I believed crushed me so
But these words I couldn't let myself think

I couldn't let myself say those words
That meant the pain would win
I bottled it up, shoved it away
Straightened my crown and raised my chin

The mascara soaked tears that streamed down my face
I decided needed to tell a different story
One of friendship and strength
One where the pain wouldn't get the glory

There will always be days where I could fall apart
But the voices remind me of my strength
Days where I'm scared I won't make it alive
But I'm reminded I need to fight this to any length

I am strong and I will win
No matter how much it rips me apart
I will remember the fire in my soul
And the grace in my heart

ABOUT THE AUTHOR

T. Michelle was born in a small, rural Idaho town, where she spent most of her life around the hustling, bustling ranching life that her family shared. Throughout various struggles in her adolescence and early adulthood, T. used writing to evoke the emotion she never knew how to convey otherwise. What started as a task planned only to say, "I did it to say I did it," Burn Unit and Yes, Dear were the first of hopefully many other writing projects planned for T. as she reminds herself why she loved writing so much.

www.ingramcontent.com/pod-product-compliance
Lightning Source LLC
LaVergne TN
LVHW090527110826
845146LV00003B/1011

* 9 7 9 8 9 8 6 4 5 1 6 5 7 *